Trauma To Triumph - A Journey To Overcoming Anxiety

Michael Ferguson

Published by Michael Ferguson, 2023.

TRAUMA TO TRIUMPH - A JOURNEY TO OVERCOMING ANXIETY

First edition. January 18, 2023.

Copyright © 2023 Michael Ferguson.

ISBN: 979-8215836989

Written by Michael Ferguson.

Table of Contents

Introduction..1

The Link Between Trauma and Anxiety 3

Understanding The Different Types Of Trauma............................5

Chapter 1: Identifying Trauma Triggers 7

Part 1: Understanding How Trauma Affects the Brain 9

Part 2: Identifying Personal Trauma Triggers 13

Part 3: Developing a Plan to Address Triggers 17

Chapter 2 – Treatment Options for Trauma 21

Part 1: Cognitive-Behavioral Therapy (CBT) 23

Part 2: Exposure Therapy 25

Part 3: Mindfulness-Based Therapy 27

Part 4: Other Treatment Options 31

Chapter 3: Coping Strategies For Managing Anxiety......................35

Part 1: Mindfulness and Meditation 37

Part 2: Journaling 41

Part 3: Exercise and Physical Activity..................................45

Chapter 4: Confronting and Processing Trauma 49

Part 1: Understanding the Stages of Trauma Processing 51

Part 2: Setting Boundaries 53

Part 3: Self-Care and Self-Compassion 55

Part 4: Setting Personal Goals 57

Chapter 5: Moving Forward 59

Part 1: Setting Personal Goals 61

Part 2: Building Resilience 63

Part 3: Maintaining Mental Health and Wellness 65

In Conclusion 67

Resources and Recommended Reading 69

Acknowledgments 71

About the Author 73

This book is dedicated to the memories of those who have been affected by trauma and to those who have lost their lives to anxiety. Your struggles have inspired me to share this knowledge and hope that it will help someone to find peace and happiness. And for my loved ones who have supported me through my own journey, thank you for always being there and for believing in me.

Introduction

Anxiety is a common mental health condition that affects millions of people worldwide. It is characterized by feelings of worry, fear, and unease that can interfere with daily activities and overall well-being. While anxiety can be caused by a variety of factors, unresolved past traumas can play a significant role in the development and maintenance of anxiety symptoms.

In this book, "Confronting Trauma: A Guide to Overcoming Anxiety," we will explore the link between trauma and anxiety, and how unresolved traumas can manifest as anxiety symptoms. We will also delve into the different types of traumas and their effects on mental health.

Through the process of identifying personal trauma triggers, understanding the available treatment options, and developing coping strategies, readers will learn how to take control of their mental health and overcome anxiety by confronting past traumas.

This book offers a unique perspective on how to address and overcome anxiety by confronting past traumas, providing readers with the tools and understanding they need to take control of their mental health and move forward in their lives. It is intended to serve as a resource for those seeking to understand and overcome anxiety related to past traumas.

The Link Between Trauma and Anxiety

Trauma is a broad term that refers to any event or experience that causes significant emotional distress. Trauma can take many forms, such as physical, emotional, or sexual abuse, neglect, accidents, natural disasters, or the loss of a loved one. Trauma can also result from ongoing stress, such as living in a war zone or experiencing poverty. Trauma can have a profound impact on an individual's mental health, and it is a major risk factor for the development of anxiety disorders. When an individual experiences a traumatic event, their body goes into a fight or flight response, which is a natural response to danger. This response is characterized by increased heart rate, rapid breathing, and heightened awareness. The fight or flight response is meant to be a temporary response to danger, but when an individual experiences trauma, their body remains in this state of heightened arousal, leading to symptoms of anxiety.

Research has shown that individuals who have experienced trauma are at a higher risk of developing anxiety disorders, such as post-traumatic stress disorder (PTSD) or generalized anxiety disorder (GAD). Trauma can also cause individuals to experience symptoms of anxiety even in the absence of a diagnosed anxiety disorder.

For example, an individual who has experienced physical abuse may develop a fear of being touched and may experience anxiety when someone comes into physical contact with them. Similarly, an individual who has experienced a natural disaster may develop a fear of storms and may experience anxiety when one is approaching. These symptoms can significantly impact the individual's quality of life and can interfere with daily activities.

Understanding the link between trauma and anxiety is important in order to effectively address and overcome anxiety symptoms. It is important to note that not everyone who experiences trauma will develop anxiety, but it is important to be aware of the potential connection.

It is also important to note that not all anxiety symptoms are related to past traumas. Anxiety can also be caused by other factors such as genetics, biology, and life events. However, for many individuals, past traumas can play a significant role in the development and maintenance of their anxiety symptoms.

Confronting past traumas can be a difficult and emotional process, but it is an important step in overcoming anxiety. By facing and processing past traumas, individuals can learn to understand and manage their anxiety symptoms. It allows individuals to take control of their mental health, and to move forward in their lives with greater peace of mind.

It's important to remember that everyone's experience with trauma and anxiety is unique, and there is no one-size-fits-all solution. However, by understanding the link between trauma and anxiety, and by learning effective coping strategies, individuals can take the first step towards overcoming anxiety and reclaiming their lives.

In the following chapters, we will delve deeper into understanding the different types of traumas, identifying personal trauma triggers, exploring treatment options, developing coping strategies, and learning how to move forward after confronting past traumas. We will also provide practical tips, exercises and worksheets to help readers apply the concepts discussed in the book to their own lives.

Understanding The Different Types Of Trauma

Trauma comes in many different forms, and each type of trauma can have a unique impact on an individual's mental health. It's important to understand the different types of traumas in order to effectively address and overcome the symptoms of anxiety that may be related to past traumas.

Some common types of traumas include:

1. Physical Trauma: Physical trauma refers to any injury or harm to the body caused by an external force. Examples of physical trauma include car accidents, physical abuse, and natural disasters.
2. Emotional Trauma: Emotional trauma refers to any emotional wound caused by an external force. Examples of emotional trauma include emotional abuse, neglect, and bullying.
3. Sexual Trauma: Sexual trauma refers to any sexual experience that causes emotional distress. Examples of sexual trauma include sexual abuse, rape, and sexual harassment.
4. Complex Trauma: Complex trauma refers to repeated or prolonged exposure to traumatic events. Examples of complex trauma include growing up in an abusive household, living in a war zone, or experiencing ongoing poverty.
5. Vicarious Trauma: Vicarious trauma refers to the emotional distress that can occur as a result of working with or helping

individuals who have experienced trauma. Examples of vicarious trauma include working as a first responder or therapist.

It's important to note that an individual's experience with trauma is unique and can be a combination of different types of traumas. It's also important to note that not all traumas are immediately visible, and some individuals may not be aware that they have experienced trauma.

In the next chapter, we will delve deeper into identifying personal trauma triggers and understanding how trauma affects the brain. We will also provide practical tips and exercises to help readers identify their own trauma triggers and develop a plan to address them.

Chapter 1: Identifying Trauma Triggers

In this chapter, we delve deeper into understanding how trauma affects the brain and the importance of identifying personal trauma triggers. The chapter begins by explaining the physiological response of the body to trauma and how this response can affect an individual's mental health.

The chapter then introduces the concept of trauma triggers, which are events or situations that can provoke memories of past traumas and trigger symptoms of anxiety. The author explains that understanding one's personal triggers is an important step in managing and overcoming anxiety symptoms related to past traumas.

The chapter also provides practical exercises and worksheets to help readers identify their own trauma triggers, such as keeping a journal of anxiety symptoms and identifying patterns or situations that tend to provoke anxiety. The author also provides guidance on how to develop a plan to address triggers, such as avoiding certain situations or developing coping strategies.

Overall, chapter one provides readers with a deeper understanding of how trauma affects the brain and the importance of identifying personal trauma triggers in managing and overcoming anxiety symptoms related to past traumas.

Part 1: Understanding How Trauma Affects the Brain

When an individual experiences a traumatic event, their body goes into a state of heightened arousal known as the fight or flight response. This response is characterized by an increase in heart rate, rapid breathing, and heightened awareness, and is meant to be a temporary response to danger. However, when an individual experiences trauma, their body remains in this state of heightened arousal, leading to symptoms of anxiety.

The fight or flight response is controlled by the sympathetic nervous system and is activated by the release of stress hormones such as adrenaline and cortisol. These hormones prepare the body for physical action by increasing blood flow to the muscles, dilating the pupils, and decreasing blood flow to the digestive system. This response is essential for survival as it allows the individual to react quickly in dangerous situations.

When an individual experiences a traumatic event, the fight or flight response is activated, but the individual may not be able to physically react to the danger. This can lead to the individual feeling trapped and helpless, and the trauma can become "stuck" in the body. Traumatic events can also cause changes in the brain, particularly in the hippocampus, the amygdala, and the prefrontal cortex.

The hippocampus is responsible for memory formation and retrieval, and trauma can cause shrinkage in this area, leading to difficulty in recalling memories or a dissociation from the traumatic event. The amygdala is responsible for processing emotions and the regulation of the fight or flight response, and trauma can cause overactivity in this area, leading to an increased sensitivity to triggers and heightened anxiety symptoms.

The prefrontal cortex is responsible for decision-making, impulse control, and the regulation of emotions, and trauma can cause changes in this area, leading to difficulty in controlling emotions and impulsive behavior.

Understanding how trauma affects the brain can help individuals understand their anxiety symptoms and develop effective coping strategies. It's important to remember that everyone's experience with trauma is unique, and the effects of trauma can vary from person to person.

Furthermore, it is important to note that trauma can also affect the brain's chemistry by altering the levels of neurotransmitters such as serotonin, dopamine and norepinephrine. This can cause changes in mood, sleep, and appetite which can affect mental health.

Additionally, trauma can lead to changes in the body's immune system, which can make the individual more susceptible to illnesses. Trauma can also lead to changes in the body's endocrine system, which can affect the way the body responds to stress.

It is also important to note that trauma can also lead to the development of disorders such as PTSD, and Complex PTSD. PTSD is a disorder that can develop after a person has experienced or witnessed a traumatic event. Symptoms of PTSD include re-experiencing the event, avoidance, and increased arousal. Complex PTSD is a form of PTSD that can develop after prolonged or repeated exposure to traumatic events. Symptoms of Complex PTSD include changes in self-perception, and difficulties in regulating emotions, and relating to others.

Understanding how trauma affects the brain is crucial in understanding and managing anxiety symptoms related to past traumas. By understanding the changes that trauma can cause in the brain, individuals can develop more effective coping strategies and work towards overcoming anxiety symptoms.

It is important to note that the effects of trauma on the brain can be long-lasting and can continue to affect an individual's mental health even after the traumatic event has ended. Trauma can affect an individual's ability to form and maintain relationships, and can cause difficulties in trust, intimacy, and communication. Trauma can also affect an individual's ability to work, study, or perform daily activities, and can cause difficulties in concentration, memory, and decision-making.

It's also important to note that trauma can affect different individuals differently. Some individuals may experience severe symptoms, while others may experience more mild symptoms. Furthermore, some individuals may recover quickly, while others may take longer to recover.

It is important for individuals to seek help if they are experiencing symptoms of anxiety related to past traumas. There are a variety of treatment options available, such as cognitive-behavioral therapy (CBT), eye movement desensitization and reprocessing (EMDR), and medication.

It's also important for individuals to take care of themselves physically and emotionally. This can include engaging in regular exercise, eating a healthy diet, getting enough sleep, and practicing relaxation techniques such as deep breathing, meditation, and yoga.

In conclusion, understanding how trauma affects the brain is crucial in understanding and managing anxiety symptoms related to past traumas. By understanding the changes that trauma can cause in the brain, individuals can develop more effective coping strategies, and work towards overcoming anxiety symptoms.

Part 2: Identifying Personal Trauma Triggers

As discussed in the previous chapter, understanding how trauma affects the brain is crucial in understanding and managing anxiety symptoms related to past traumas. Another important step in managing anxiety symptoms is identifying personal trauma triggers.

Trauma triggers are events or situations that can provoke memories of past traumas and trigger symptoms of anxiety. Triggers can be different for each individual and can include things like certain sounds, smells, or sights that remind the individual of the traumatic event. Triggers can also include certain situations such as being in a crowded place, or being in a relationship that reminds the individual of an abusive relationship.

Identifying personal trauma triggers can be a difficult process, but it is an important step in managing and overcoming anxiety symptoms related to past traumas. By identifying personal triggers, individuals can take steps to avoid or manage those triggers and develop coping strategies to help them manage the symptoms of anxiety when they are triggered.

One way to identify personal trauma triggers is to keep a journal of anxiety symptoms. Individuals can record the date, time, and situation in which they experienced the symptoms, and look for patterns or situations that tend to provoke anxiety. It's also important to note any physical symptoms that may accompany the anxiety symptoms, such as heart palpitations, sweating, or shaking.

Another way to identify personal trauma triggers is to work with a therapist or counselor. A therapist or counselor can help individuals explore their past traumas and help them identify situations or events that may be triggering their anxiety symptoms.

Once personal trauma triggers have been identified, individuals can develop a plan to address them. This can include avoiding certain situations or developing coping strategies such as deep breathing, meditation, or visualization to manage the symptoms of anxiety when they are triggered.

It's important to remember that identifying personal trauma triggers is a process, and it may take some time to identify all of the triggers. It's also important to remember that triggers can change over time, and it's important to continue to monitor and address them as they arise.

Additionally, it is important to note that not all triggers are obvious or easy to identify. Sometimes, individuals may not be aware that a certain situation or event is triggering their anxiety symptoms. It may take some time and self-reflection to identify all of the personal triggers. It's also important to remember that triggers can change over time, and it's important to continue to monitor and address them as they arise.

It's also important to acknowledge that not all triggers can be avoided, and it's important to learn how to cope with triggers that can't be avoided. This may include developing coping strategies such as deep breathing, meditation, or visualization to manage the symptoms of anxiety when they are triggered.

It's important to remember that identifying personal trauma triggers is a process and it may take some time to identify all of the triggers. It's also important to remember that triggers can change over time, and it's important to continue to monitor and address them as they arise.

TRAUMA TO TRIUMPH - A JOURNEY TO OVERCOMING ANXIETY

In summary, identifying personal trauma triggers is an important step in managing and overcoming anxiety symptoms related to past traumas. By identifying personal triggers, individuals can take steps to avoid or manage those triggers and develop coping strategies to help them manage the symptoms of anxiety when they are triggered. In the next chapter, we will delve deeper into exploring treatment options for managing and overcoming anxiety symptoms related to past traumas.

Part 3: Developing a Plan to Address Triggers

Once personal trauma triggers have been identified, the next step is to develop a plan to address them. This can include taking steps to avoid or manage those triggers and developing coping strategies to help manage the symptoms of anxiety when they are triggered.

Avoiding Triggers: One way to address triggers is to avoid them. This may include avoiding certain places, people, or situations that may trigger anxiety symptoms. For example, if a certain sound is a trigger, an individual may avoid places where that sound is likely to be heard. If a certain person is a trigger, an individual may choose to avoid contact with that person.

Managing Triggers: Sometimes, it's not possible to avoid triggers entirely. In these cases, it's important to learn how to manage the triggers. This may include developing coping strategies such as deep breathing, meditation, or visualization to manage the symptoms of anxiety when they are triggered. Additionally, it can be helpful to have a support system in place, whether that's a therapist, counselor, or a trusted friend or family member, to talk through feelings or feelings of anxiety when triggers occur.

Developing Coping Strategies: Developing coping strategies is an important step in managing and overcoming anxiety symptoms related to past traumas. Coping strategies can include deep breathing exercises, meditation, yoga, or visualization. These strategies can help individuals manage the symptoms of anxiety when they are triggered. It's important to find a coping strategy that works for the individual and to practice it regularly.

It's also important to remember that triggers can change over time, and it's important to continue to monitor and address them as they arise. This may mean revisiting the plan and adjusting it as needed.

In summary, developing a plan to address triggers is an important step in managing and overcoming anxiety symptoms related to past traumas. By taking steps to avoid or manage triggers and developing coping strategies, individuals can better manage the symptoms of anxiety when they are triggered. It's important to remember that triggers can change over time, and it's important to continue to monitor and address them as they arise.

It's also important to note that addressing triggers is not a one-time process, it's an ongoing process that requires patience and persistence. It's normal to have setbacks and to experience anxiety symptoms even when triggers have been identified and addressed. It's important to be kind and patient with oneself and to remember that recovery is a journey.

Another important aspect of addressing triggers is learning how to recognize and manage the physical symptoms of anxiety. This includes learning how to recognize the signs of an anxiety attack such as rapid heartbeat, sweating, and shaking, and learning how to calm the body down through breathing exercises and relaxation techniques.

It's also important to remember that addressing triggers is not only about avoiding or managing the triggers but also about learning how to manage the emotions associated with the triggers. This may include learning how to identify and express feelings in a healthy way and learning how to develop healthy coping mechanisms for dealing with difficult emotions.

In conclusion, addressing triggers is an important step in managing and overcoming anxiety symptoms related to past traumas. By identifying personal triggers, developing a plan to address them, and developing coping strategies, individuals can better manage the symptoms of anxiety when they are triggered. It's important to remember that addressing triggers is an ongoing process that requires patience and persistence, and that recovery is a journey.

Chapter 2 – Treatment Options for Trauma

This chapter provides an overview of the different treatment options available for individuals who have experienced trauma. It covers different forms of therapy, medication, and alternative therapies that are used to treat trauma-related conditions such as anxiety, PTSD, and Complex PTSD.

Cognitive-behavioral therapy (CBT) is a widely accepted and effective form of treatment for individuals who have experienced trauma. It is a form of psychotherapy that focuses on the relationship between an individual's thoughts, emotions, and behaviors. CBT helps individuals to identify and change negative patterns of thinking and behavior that contribute to the development of anxiety and other mental health disorders related to past traumas.

Other forms of therapy that are used to treat trauma include Eye Movement Desensitization and Reprocessing (EMDR), Prolonged Exposure Therapy (PE), and Acceptance and Commitment Therapy (ACT).

Medication such as antidepressants, anti-anxiety medication, and antipsychotics can also be used to treat trauma-related conditions. However, it's important to note that medication should be used in conjunction with therapy, and it should be prescribed and monitored by a qualified healthcare professional.

Alternative therapies such as yoga, meditation, and acupuncture may also be helpful in managing symptoms of trauma.

It's important to note that the treatment options for trauma will vary depending on the individual and the specific trauma they experienced. It may take some time and trial and error to find the right treatment for an individual, but with the help of a qualified health-care professional, it is possible to manage and overcome the symptoms of trauma.

22

Part 1: Cognitive-Behavioral Therapy (CBT)

Cognitive-behavioral therapy (CBT) is a widely accepted and effective form of treatment for individuals who have experienced trauma. It is a form of psychotherapy that focuses on the relationship between an individual's thoughts, emotions, and behaviors. CBT helps individuals to identify and change negative patterns of thinking and behavior that contribute to the development of anxiety and other mental health disorders related to past traumas.

During CBT, the therapist will work with the individual to identify negative thoughts and beliefs about themselves, others, and the world that contribute to anxiety symptoms. The therapist will then help the individual to challenge these negative thoughts and beliefs with evidence-based strategies.

Exposure therapy is also a key component of CBT for trauma. This technique involves gradually exposing the individual to traumatic memory or triggers in a safe and controlled environment. This helps to reduce the fear and avoidance associated with trauma, which can lead to a decrease in anxiety symptoms.

In addition to these techniques, relaxation and stress management techniques such as deep breathing, progressive muscle relaxation, and mindfulness will be taught to help individuals cope with anxiety symptoms and triggers. A safety plan will also be developed to help individuals manage anxiety symptoms and triggers that may occur outside of therapy sessions.

CBT has been shown to be effective in treating anxiety disorders related to past traumas and it can help individuals understand their symptoms and develop strategies to manage and overcome them. It's important to note that CBT is not a one-size-fits-all approach, and it may take time for an individual to see improvement but with time and effort, it can be a powerful tool in managing and overcoming anxiety symptoms related to past traumas.

It's also important to note that CBT is not a quick fix, it requires commitment and effort from the individual. It may take several sessions before an individual starts to see improvement, but with time and effort, the results can be long-lasting.

It's also important to note that CBT should be conducted by a licensed therapist or mental health professional who has experience and training in treating trauma. They will be able to provide guidance and support during the therapeutic process.

In conclusion, CBT is a widely accepted and effective form of treatment for individuals who have experienced trauma. It helps individuals to identify and change negative patterns of thinking and behavior that contribute to the development of anxiety and other mental health disorders related to past traumas. With time and effort, it can be a powerful tool in managing and overcoming anxiety symptoms related to past traumas.

Part 2: Exposure Therapy

Exposure therapy is a form of cognitive-behavioral therapy (CBT) that is commonly used to treat anxiety disorders, including those related to past traumas. It is based on the principle that by gradually exposing an individual to traumatic memory or triggers in a safe and controlled environment, the individual can learn to manage and reduce the fear and avoidance associated with the trauma.

Exposure therapy typically involves creating a hierarchy of feared situations, starting with the least anxiety-provoking and gradually working up to the most anxiety-provoking. The individual will then be gradually exposed to each item on the hierarchy until they can tolerate the most feared situation without experiencing significant distress.

During exposure therapy, the individual will be guided by a therapist who will provide support and guidance throughout the process. The therapist will also teach coping strategies such as deep breathing and progressive muscle relaxation to help the individual manage any anxiety symptoms that may arise during exposure.

Exposure therapy can be done in a variety of ways, including in vivo (in real life), imaginal (in the mind), and virtual reality exposure therapy. The method used will depend on the individual's specific trauma and needs.

Exposure therapy has been shown to be effective in treating anxiety disorders related to past traumas, including post-traumatic stress disorder (PTSD). It allows individuals to confront and manage their fears in a safe and controlled environment, leading to a decrease in anxiety symptoms and an improvement in overall quality of life.

It's important to note that exposure therapy should only be conducted by a licensed therapist or mental health professional who has experience and training in treating trauma. It's also important to note that exposure therapy is not a one-time treatment, it's an ongoing process that requires patience and persistence.

Additionally, it is important to note that exposure therapy may not be suitable for everyone, particularly if the individual has experienced severe and complex trauma. In such cases, other forms of therapy such as Eye Movement Desensitization and Reprocessing (EMDR) may be more appropriate.

It's also important to remember that exposure therapy can be difficult and emotionally challenging, but it's important to have an open and honest conversation with the therapist about any concerns or difficulties that may arise during the process.

It's also important for the individual to be prepared for the possibility of experiencing some level of distress during the exposure process. The therapist will be there to provide support and guidance, but it's important for the individual to be open to the process and willing to push through any discomfort in order to achieve the ultimate goal of managing and reducing anxiety symptoms.

It's also important to remember that exposure therapy should be part of a comprehensive treatment plan that includes other forms of therapy, medication, and self-care practices such as exercise, healthy eating, and adequate sleep.

It's important to note that recovery from trauma takes time and patience, but with the right treatment, support, and effort, it is possible to manage and overcome the symptoms of trauma.

Part 3: Mindfulness-Based Therapy

Mindfulness-based therapy is a form of therapy that incorporates mindfulness practices to help individuals manage their thoughts, emotions, and behaviors related to past traumas. Mindfulness is the practice of being present in the moment and paying attention to one's thoughts, emotions, and physical sensations without judgment. Mindfulness-based therapy typically includes several key components:

1. Mindfulness practices: The therapist will teach the individual mindfulness practices such as meditation, yoga, and body scan to help them focus on the present moment and develop a greater awareness of their thoughts, emotions, and physical sensations.

2. Acceptance and non-judgment: The therapist will help the individual develop an accepting and non-judgmental attitude towards their thoughts, emotions, and physical sensations. This can help the individual to better manage and cope with their symptoms.

3. Emotion regulation: The therapist will teach the individual techniques to regulate their emotions, such as mindfulness of emotions, self-compassion, and cognitive reappraisal.

4. Trauma-specific interventions: The therapist will incorporate trauma-specific interventions such as imagery and writing exercises to help the individual process their trauma in a safe and controlled environment.

Mindfulness-based therapy has been shown to be effective in treating anxiety disorders related to past traumas. It can help individuals to develop a greater awareness of their thoughts, emotions, and physical sensations, which can lead to a reduction in anxiety symptoms and an improvement in overall quality of life.

It's important to note that mindfulness-based therapy should be conducted by a licensed therapist or mental health professional who has experience and training in treating trauma. It's also important to note that mindfulness-based therapy is not a one-time treatment, it's an ongoing process that requires patience and persistence.

In addition, mindfulness-based therapy can be used as an adjunct to other forms of therapy such as cognitive-behavioral therapy (CBT) and exposure therapy. Mindfulness practices can help individuals to better manage and cope with their symptoms during the exposure process.

It's also important to note that mindfulness-based therapy may not be suitable for everyone, particularly if the individual has experienced severe and complex trauma. In such cases, other forms of therapy such as Eye Movement Desensitization and Reprocessing (EMDR) may be more appropriate.

It's also important to remember that mindfulness-based therapy can be difficult and emotionally challenging, but it's important to have an open and honest conversation with the therapist about any concerns or difficulties that may arise during the process.

It's also important for the individual to be prepared for the possibility of experiencing some level of distress during the mindfulness practices. The therapist will be there to provide support and guidance, but it's important for the individual to be open to the process and willing to push through any discomfort in order to achieve the ultimate goal of managing and reducing anxiety symptoms.

TRAUMA TO TRIUMPH - A JOURNEY TO OVERCOMING ANXIETY

It's also important to remember that mindfulness-based therapy should be part of a comprehensive treatment plan that includes other forms of therapy, medication, and self-care practices such as exercise, healthy eating, and adequate sleep.

It's important to note that recovery from trauma takes time and patience, but with the right treatment, support, and effort, it is possible to manage and overcome the symptoms of trauma. Mindfulness-based therapy can play an important role in this process by helping individuals to develop a greater awareness of their thoughts, emotions, and physical sensations, and to develop skills to manage them in a more effective way.

Part 4: Other Treatment Options

In addition to cognitive-behavioral therapy (CBT), exposure therapy, and mindfulness-based therapy, there are other treatment options available for individuals who have experienced trauma. These include:

1. Eye Movement Desensitization and Reprocessing (EMDR): This is a form of therapy that uses eye movements, sounds, or taps to help the individual process traumatic memories and reduce the distress associated with them.

2. Prolonged Exposure therapy (PE): This is a form of CBT that involves gradually exposing the individual to traumatic memories or triggers in a safe and controlled environment.

3. Acceptance and Commitment Therapy (ACT): This is a form of therapy that focuses on helping the individual to accept and make peace with their trauma and to commit to taking action to improve their quality of life.

4. Medication: Antidepressants, anti-anxiety medication, and antipsychotics can be used to treat trauma-related conditions. However, it's important to note that medication should be used in conjunction with therapy and should be prescribed and monitored by a qualified healthcare professional.

5. Alternative therapies: Yoga, meditation, acupuncture, and other alternative therapies may also be helpful in managing symptoms of trauma.

It's important to note that the treatment options for trauma will vary depending on the individual and the specific trauma they experienced. It may take some time and trial and error to find the right treatment for an individual, but with the help of a qualified healthcare professional, it is possible to manage and overcome the symptoms of trauma.

It's also important to remember that recovery from trauma is an ongoing process and that it may take time and patience to find the right treatment and to see improvement. It's important to have realistic expectations and to be patient with yourself and your progress.

It's important to note that some people may also find relief from trauma through the use of cannabis-based products such as CBD (cannabidiol) and THC (tetrahydrocannabinol). These compounds have been shown to have anti-anxiety and anti-inflammatory properties, which may help to alleviate symptoms of trauma. However, it's important to note that more research is needed in this area, and it's important to consult with a qualified healthcare professional before using any cannabis-based products for the treatment of trauma.

Recently, some doctors have been prescribing psychedelics such as Ketamine and LSD for the treatment of trauma. These substances are thought to have the potential to help individuals to process traumatic memories and to reduce the distress associated with them. However, it's important to note that the use of psychedelics is still considered experimental, and more research is needed in this area. It's also important to note that psychedelics are illegal in many places and should only be used under the supervision of a qualified healthcare professional.

In conclusion, there are various treatment options available for individuals who have experienced trauma. Cognitive-behavioral therapy (CBT), exposure therapy, and mindfulness-based therapy are widely recognized as effective treatments for trauma. Other options such as Eye Movement Desensitization and Reprocessing (EMDR), Prolonged Exposure therapy (PE), Acceptance and Commitment Therapy (ACT), Medication and alternative therapies may also be helpful in managing symptoms of trauma. It's important to remember that recovery from trauma is an ongoing process and that it may take time and patience to find the right treatment and to see improvement. It's important to consult with a qualified healthcare professional to determine the best course of treatment for you. Additionally, some people may find relief through the use of cannabis-based products or psychedelics, but it's important to consult with a qualified healthcare professional before using these methods. Remember that with the right treatment, support, and effort, it is possible to manage and overcome the symptoms of trauma.

Chapter 3: Coping Strategies For Managing Anxiety

In this chapter coping strategies for managing anxiety focuses on providing practical and effective strategies for managing anxiety symptoms that arise as a result of past traumas. The chapter provides detailed information on various coping strategies that individuals can use to manage anxiety in their daily lives, such as deep breathing exercises, progressive muscle relaxation, and mindfulness practices. The chapter also includes information on how to develop a self-care plan and how to identify and challenge negative thoughts and beliefs.

Additionally, the chapter includes information on how to manage triggers, such as developing a plan for coping with triggers and using grounding techniques. The chapter also covers the importance of building a support system, such as seeking out friends and family for support and finding a therapist or counselor who has experience in treating trauma.

Throughout the chapter, the reader will find real-life examples and practical exercises to help them apply these coping strategies in their daily lives. The chapter concludes by emphasizing the importance of patience and persistence in the process of managing anxiety symptoms and overcoming past traumas.

Part 1: Mindfulness and Meditation

Mindfulness and meditation are powerful tools for managing anxiety symptoms that arise as a result of past traumas. Mindfulness is the practice of being present in the moment and paying attention to one's thoughts, emotions, and physical sensations without judgment. Meditation is a technique that can be used to achieve a state of mindfulness.

There are various forms of mindfulness and meditation practices that can be used to manage anxiety, such as:

1. Body scan: This is a form of mindfulness meditation that involves focusing on each part of the body and noticing any sensations or feelings.
2. Sitting meditation: This is a form of mindfulness meditation that involves sitting in a comfortable position and focusing on the breath.
3. Walking meditation: This is a form of mindfulness meditation that involves walking at a slow pace and focusing on the sensation of the feet on the ground.
4. Yoga: Yoga is a form of mindfulness meditation that involves movement, breath control, and meditation.
5. Guided meditation: This is a form of mindfulness meditation that involves listening to a recorded meditation or a live guide.

It's important to note that mindfulness and meditation practices should be used in conjunction with other forms of therapy and should be practiced regularly. It's also important to note that mindfulness and meditation may be difficult and emotionally challenging, but it's important to have an open and honest conversation with a therapist about any concerns or difficulties that may arise during the process.

It's also important to remember that mindfulness and meditation should be part of a comprehensive treatment plan that includes other forms of therapy, medication, and self-care practices such as exercise, healthy eating, and adequate sleep.

One of the benefits of mindfulness and meditation is that it can help individuals to develop a greater awareness of their thoughts, emotions, and physical sensations. This awareness can help individuals to recognize when they are becoming anxious and to take steps to manage their symptoms. Mindfulness and meditation can also help to reduce the intensity of anxiety symptoms and to promote relaxation.

It's also important to note that mindfulness and meditation can help individuals to develop a greater sense of self-compassion and self-acceptance. This can be particularly helpful for individuals who have experienced trauma, as they may be hard on themselves and blame themselves for what has happened.

To get the most out of mindfulness and meditation, it's important to practice regularly and to be patient with yourself. It can take time to develop the skills necessary to be mindful and to meditate effectively. It's also important to note that mindfulness and meditation may not be suitable for everyone, particularly if the individual has experienced severe and complex trauma. In such cases, other forms of therapy such as Eye Movement Desensitization and Reprocessing (EMDR) may be more appropriate.

It's also important to remember that mindfulness and meditation are not a cure for anxiety and trauma, but rather tools that can be used to manage symptoms. It's important to work with a qualified healthcare professional to develop a comprehensive treatment plan that addresses the root causes of anxiety and trauma.

In conclusion, mindfulness and meditation are powerful tools for managing anxiety symptoms that arise as a result of past traumas. There are various forms of mindfulness and meditation practices that can be used, such as body scan, sitting meditation, walking meditation, yoga, and guided meditation. These practices can help individuals to develop a greater awareness of their thoughts, emotions, and physical sensations, and to take steps to manage their symptoms. Mindfulness and meditation can also help to reduce the intensity of anxiety symptoms and to promote relaxation. However, it is important to practice regularly and to be patient with yourself. It's also important to note that mindfulness and meditation may not be suitable for everyone, particularly if the individual has experienced severe and complex trauma. It's important to work with a qualified healthcare professional to develop a comprehensive treatment plan that addresses the root causes of anxiety and trauma. Mindfulness and meditation should be used as a part of a comprehensive treatment plan that includes other forms of therapy, medication, and self-care practices such as exercise, healthy eating, and adequate sleep.

Part 2: Journaling

Journaling is a powerful tool for managing anxiety symptoms that arise as a result of past traumas. Journaling is the practice of writing down one's thoughts, feelings, and experiences in a diary or notebook. It can be used as a way to process and understand one's thoughts and emotions, and to gain a better understanding of oneself and one's experiences.

There are various forms of journaling that can be used to manage anxiety, such as:

1. Stream of consciousness writing: This is a form of journaling that involves writing down whatever comes to mind without editing or censoring oneself.
2. Gratitude journaling: This is a form of journaling that involves writing down things that one is grateful for on a daily basis.
3. Reflection journaling: This is a form of journaling that involves reflecting on one's experiences, thoughts, and emotions, and analyzing how they may be related to one's anxiety.
4. Mind mapping: This is a form of journaling that involves creating a visual representation of one's thoughts, feelings, and experiences.
5. Art journaling: This is a form of journaling that involves using art and creative expression as a way to process and understand one's thoughts and emotions.

It's important to note that journaling should be used in conjunction with other forms of therapy and should be practiced regularly. It's also important to note that journaling may be difficult and emotionally challenging, but it's important to have an open and honest conversation with a therapist about any concerns or difficulties that may arise during the process.

Journaling can be particularly helpful for individuals who have experienced trauma, as it can provide a safe space to process and understand their thoughts and emotions. It can also help individuals to identify patterns in their thoughts and emotions and to develop a greater understanding of their triggers. Journaling can also be helpful for individuals who have difficulty expressing themselves verbally, as it allows them to communicate their thoughts and feelings in a safe and non-judgmental way.

To get the most out of journaling, it's important to practice regularly and to be honest with oneself. It can take time to develop the skills necessary to journal effectively. It's also important to remember that journaling should be part of a comprehensive treatment plan that includes other forms of therapy, medication, and self-care practices such as exercise, healthy eating, and adequate sleep.

One of the benefits of journaling is that it can help individuals to process and understand their thoughts and emotions. This can be particularly helpful for individuals who have experienced trauma, as it can provide a safe space to process and understand their thoughts and emotions. Journaling can also help individuals to identify patterns in their thoughts and emotions and to develop a greater understanding of their triggers.

A journaling exercise that can be helpful for individuals with anxiety and for confronting past traumas is to write a letter to the traumatic event or person. In this letter, the individual can express their thoughts, feelings, and emotions towards the event or person. They can also write down their forgiveness if they feel ready, or write their feelings of anger, pain and resentment if they are not ready yet. This exercise allows the individual to process their thoughts and emotions in a safe and non-judgmental way and can be a powerful tool in the healing process.

It's important to remember that journaling is not a substitute for professional therapy and should be used in conjunction with other forms of therapy. It's also important to consult with a qualified healthcare professional to determine if journaling is appropriate for you and if so, how to use it effectively in your healing process.

In conclusion, journaling is a powerful tool for managing anxiety symptoms that arise as a result of past traumas. There are various forms of journaling that can be used, such as stream of consciousness writing, gratitude journaling, reflection journaling, mind mapping, and art journaling. Journaling can be particularly helpful for individuals who have experienced trauma, as it can provide a safe space to process and understand their thoughts and emotions, and to develop a greater understanding of their triggers. To get the most out of journaling, it's important to practice regularly and to be honest with oneself. It's also important to remember that journaling should be part of a comprehensive treatment plan that includes other forms of therapy, medication, and self-care practices such as exercise, healthy eating, and adequate sleep.

Part 3: Exercise and Physical Activity

Exercise and physical activity are powerful tools for managing anxiety symptoms that arise as a result of past traumas. Regular exercise can help to reduce the symptoms of anxiety, such as tension, restlessness, and irritability. It can also help to improve mood, reduce stress, and promote relaxation.

There are various forms of exercise and physical activity that can be used to manage anxiety, such as:

1. Aerobic exercise: This includes activities such as running, cycling, swimming, and dancing. Aerobic exercise can help to increase heart rate and promote the release of endorphins, which can help to improve mood and reduce anxiety.

2. Strength training: This includes activities such as weightlifting and resistance training. Strength training can help to improve muscle tone and increase feelings of self-esteem and self-confidence.

3. Yoga: This includes a combination of physical poses, breathing exercises, and meditation. Yoga can help to promote relaxation, reduce stress, and improve overall well-being.

4. Outdoor activities: This includes activities such as hiking, walking, and gardening. These activities can provide an opportunity to connect with nature, which can help to reduce stress and improve mood.

It's important to note that the type of exercise and physical activity that is best for managing anxiety will depend on the individual. It's also important to consult with a qualified healthcare professional to determine if exercise and physical activity are appropriate for you and if so, what type of exercise and physical activity would be best for you.

Exercise and physical activity can be particularly helpful for individuals who have experienced trauma, as it can provide a sense of control over one's body and can help to reduce feelings of helplessness. It can also be helpful for individuals who have difficulty expressing themselves verbally, as it allows them to communicate their thoughts and feelings in a safe and non-judgmental way.

To get the most out of exercise and physical activity, it's important to practice regularly and to be patient with yourself. It can take time to develop the skills necessary to exercise effectively. It's also important to remember that exercise and physical activity should be part of a comprehensive treatment plan that includes other forms of therapy, medication, and self-care practices such as healthy eating, adequate sleep, and journaling.

In conclusion, exercise and physical activity can play a crucial role in the healing process for individuals who have experienced trauma and are struggling with anxiety. Regular physical activity can have a positive impact on both physical and mental health. It can help to reduce symptoms of anxiety and depression, improve mood, and promote overall well-being. It's important to find activities that you enjoy, and to start with a manageable level of intensity and gradually increase the level of difficulty over time. It's also important to listen to your body and not to push yourself too hard. Exercise and physical activity should be used as a part of a comprehensive treatment plan that includes other forms of therapy, medication, and self-care practices such as healthy eating, adequate sleep, and journaling. Remember, it's important to consult with a qualified healthcare professional to determine if exercise and physical activity are appropriate for you and to develop an exercise plan that is tailored to your needs.

Chapter 4: Confronting and Processing Trauma

This chapter focuses on the importance of confronting and processing past traumas in order to manage and reduce symptoms of anxiety. The chapter begins by discussing the link between trauma and anxiety and the importance of understanding the different types of traumas. It then goes on to explore various techniques for confronting and processing past traumas, including cognitive-behavioral therapy, exposure therapy, and mindfulness-based therapy.

The chapter also delves into the different coping strategies that can be used to manage anxiety symptoms, including journaling, mindfulness and meditation, and exercise and physical activity. It also provides tips for identifying personal trauma triggers and developing a plan to address them. The chapter concludes with an emphasis on the importance of a comprehensive treatment plan that includes therapy, medication, and self-care practices.

This chapter is particularly useful for individuals who have experienced past traumas and are struggling with anxiety symptoms. It provides a comprehensive overview of the different types of traumas, the link between trauma and anxiety, and the various treatment options and coping strategies that are available. The chapter also provides practical tips and exercises that can be used to manage and reduce symptoms of anxiety. It's important to remember that healing from past traumas takes time and effort, and it's important to consult with a qualified healthcare professional to determine the best course of treatment.

Part 1: Understanding the Stages of Trauma Processing

When an individual experiences a traumatic event, it can take time for them to process and make sense of what has happened. Understanding the stages of trauma processing can help individuals to understand their own healing journey and to have realistic expectations for their recovery.

The first stage of trauma processing is the acute stage, which occurs immediately after A traumatic event. During this stage, individuals may experience symptoms of shock and disbelief, such as feelings of numbness, confusion, and disconnection. They may also experience intense feelings of fear and helplessness.

The second stage is the intermediate stage, which typically lasts for several weeks to several months after the traumatic event. During this stage, individuals may experience symptoms of anxiety, depression, guilt, and shame. They may also begin to experience flashbacks and nightmares related to the traumatic event.

The third stage is the long-term stage, which can last for months or even years after the traumatic event. During this stage, individuals may continue to experience symptoms of anxiety, depression, and PTSD. However, they may also begin to make progress in their healing and may begin to experience a sense of resolution and closure related to the traumatic event.

It's important to note that not everyone will experience these stages in a linear fashion, and some people may experience symptoms from previous stages even after they have progressed to the next stage. Additionally, everyone's healing process is unique and can be affected by different factors such as the nature of the trauma, the individual's coping mechanisms and support systems, and the availability of professional help.

It's important to understand that trauma processing is a journey, and it's important to be patient with oneself. It's also important to seek professional help if needed, and to also surround oneself with support and care from loved ones

Part 2: Setting Boundaries

Confronting and processing past traumas can be a difficult and emotional process. Setting boundaries is an important step in protecting oneself during this process. Boundaries help to create physical and emotional space, which can help to reduce feelings of overwhelm and anxiety.

When setting boundaries, it's important to consider what feels safe and comfortable for oneself. This may mean limiting contact with certain people or places that trigger memories of the traumatic event, or it may mean setting limits on the amount of time spent discussing the traumatic event with others.

It's also important to set boundaries with oneself. This may mean setting limits on the amount of time spent thinking about or revisiting the traumatic event, or it may mean setting limits on the amount of time spent engaging in self-destructive behaviors.

It's crucial to keep in mind that seeking assistance is not a sign of weakness, but rather a demonstration of courage. Trauma can be intense and hard to process on one's own. Being open to seeking help and support from friends, loved ones and professionals is crucial to the healing process. It may be challenging to be vulnerable and ask for help, however it's essential to remember that it is a necessary step in overcoming the effects of trauma and setting healthy boundaries. Finding a therapist or counselor with experience in working with trauma can also be beneficial. Many people find that therapy or counseling, combined with support from loved ones, can be an important tool in helping them to process and heal from their traumas.

It's important to communicate these boundaries to others, in a clear and assertive manner. This can be difficult, as it may mean saying "no" or standing up for oneself in situations where one may have previously felt uncomfortable. However, setting boundaries is a crucial step in protecting oneself during the trauma processing journey.

It's also important to remember that boundaries can change over time, and that it's okay to adjust them as needed. As an individual begins to heal and make progress, boundaries may become more flexible. It's important to be aware of one's own needs and to make adjustments as needed.

In conclusion, setting boundaries is an important step in protecting oneself during the process of confronting and processing past traumas. It's important to set boundaries between oneself and others, doing so in a clear and assertive manner. Remember that boundaries can change over time and it's important to be aware of one's own needs and to make adjustments as needed.

Part 3: Self-Care and Self-Compassion

Herb Carnegie, a Canadian ice hockey player and coach, once said, "You must be your own best friend." This quote is a powerful reminder of the importance of self-care and self-compassion when it comes to healing from trauma.

Self-care is about taking the time physically and emotionally. This may include things like getting enough sleep, eating well, engaging in regular physical activity, and practicing stress-reduction techniques such as yoga or meditation. Self-care also includes setting boundaries, as mentioned earlier, and taking time for oneself to relax and recharge.

Self-compassion is about treating oneself with the same kindness, concern, and forgiveness that one would offer to a good friend. This means being understanding and non-judgmental of oneself and recognizing that everyone makes mistakes and has difficult moments. Self-compassion also means being patient with oneself during the healing process and not expecting immediate results.

When it comes to healing from trauma, self-care and self-compassion are essential. It's important to remember that healing takes time and that it's okay to take things one step at a time. It's also important to remember that healing is a journey, not a destination. By practicing self-care and self-compassion, individuals can create a safe and supportive environment for themselves, which can help to foster healing and growth.

In conclusion, self-care and self-compassion are crucial elements of healing from trauma. By following Herb Carnegie's advice and being one's own best friend, individuals can create a safe and supportive environment for themselves, which can help to foster healing and growth. It's important to remember that healing takes time and that it's okay to take things one step at a time, and that healing is a journey, not a destination.

Part 4: Setting Personal Goals

The healing process is not a destination but a journey, and it's important to have a plan for moving forward. One way to do this is by setting personal goals. These goals can help to provide a sense of direction and purpose, and they can help to keep an individual motivated and focused on their healing journey.

When setting personal goals, it's important to start with something small and manageable. It's also important to be realistic and to consider one's own abilities and limitations. Goals should be specific, measurable, achievable, relevant, and time bound.

For example, a goal might be to attend therapy or counseling once a week for the next month, or to spend 15 minutes each day practicing mindfulness or meditation. Another goal might be to read one self-help book per month, or to spend 30 minutes each day engaging in physical activity.

It's also important to remember that goals may change over time, and that it's okay to adjust them as needed. It's important to be flexible and to be willing to change course if something isn't working.

Dale Carnegie, the American writer and lecturer, once said, "The successful person is the individual who forms the habit of doing what the failing person doesn't like to do." This quote is a powerful reminder of the importance of setting personal goals and taking action to achieve them.

When setting personal goals, it's important to take a holistic approach, focusing not just on physical or mental goals, but also on emotional and spiritual goals. This might include goals related to self-care, self-compassion, and emotional well-being, as well as goals related to career, relationships, and personal growth.

To effectively set personal goals, it is important to first set a clear and specific objective. Break down that objective into smaller and measurable goals and set a deadline for each of them. This will provide a clear roadmap for progress and allow you to track your progress.

Another important step is to take consistent and persistent action towards your goals. It's not enough to simply set a goal, it's important to take action and put in the necessary work to achieve it. This might include things like attending therapy or counseling, practicing self-care and self-compassion, or engaging in physical activity.

Finally, it's important to be flexible and adaptable in the face of obstacles and setbacks. As Dale Carnegie said, "Success is getting what you want. Happiness is wanting what you get." By focusing on progress and growth rather than perfection, you can maintain a positive mindset and keep moving forward, even in the face of challenges.

In conclusion, setting personal goals is about taking a holistic approach, setting clear and specific objectives, taking consistent and persistent action towards those goals, and being flexible and adaptable in the face of obstacles and setbacks. By following these principles, individuals can achieve their goals, and ultimately find success and happiness in the process.

Chapter 5: Moving Forward

Chapter 5: Moving Forward is the final chapter of the book, which aims to provide readers with practical tools and strategies for moving forward after confronting and processing past traumas. This chapter focuses on the importance of self-care, self-compassion and setting healthy boundaries. It also provides guidance on how to continue the healing process and maintain progress in the future.

In Part 1, the chapter highlights the importance of self-care and self-compassion, and how it can aid in the healing process. The section provides tips and strategies for self-care, including exercise, mindfulness and meditation, and journaling.

Part 2 focuses on the importance of setting healthy boundaries, both with oneself and others. It provides guidance on how to communicate and maintain these boundaries, and how to adjust them as needed.

In the final part of the chapter, the book provides guidance on how to maintain progress and continue the healing process in the future. This includes continuing therapy or counseling, seeking support from loved ones and friends, and practicing self-care and self-compassion on an ongoing basis.

Overall, Chapter 5: Moving Forward provides readers with practical tools and strategies for moving forward after confronting and processing past traumas. It emphasizes the importance of self-care, self-compassion, and setting healthy boundaries in the healing process, and provides guidance on how to continue the healing process and maintain progress in the future.

Part 1: Setting Personal Goals

Dale Carnegie, the American writer and lecturer, once said, "The successful person is the individual who forms the habit of doing what the failing person doesn't like to do." This quote is a powerful reminder of the importance of setting personal goals and taking action to achieve them.

The healing process is not a destination but a journey, and it's important to have a plan for moving forward. One way to do this is by setting personal goals. These goals can help to provide a sense of direction and purpose, and they can help to keep an individual motivated and focused on their healing journey.

When setting personal goals, it's important to start with something small and manageable. It's also important to be realistic and to consider one's own abilities and limitations. Goals should be specific, measurable, achievable, relevant, and time bound.

For example, a goal might be to attend therapy or counseling once a week for the next month, or to spend 15 minutes each day practicing mindfulness or meditation. Another goal might be to read one self-help book per month, or to spend 30 minutes each day engaging in physical activity.

It's also important to remember that goals may change over time, and that it's okay to adjust them as needed. It's important to be flexible and to be willing to change course if something isn't working.

In conclusion, setting personal goals can be an important tool for moving forward and maintaining progress on the healing journey. It's important to start small, be realistic, and to have a plan for achieving those goals. Remember that goals may change over time, and it's important to be flexible and to adjust them as needed.

Part 2: Building Resilience

Resilience is the ability to bounce back from adversity and to cope with difficult situations. It's an essential trait to have when it comes to healing from trauma and moving forward. In this section, we will explore ways to build resilience and to develop the skills necessary to cope with difficult situations.

One of the most important ways to build resilience is through self-care and self-compassion. By taking care of oneself, both physically and emotionally, individuals can build a strong foundation of well-being, which can help to buffer against the effects of stress and trauma. This might include things like getting enough sleep, eating well, engaging in regular physical activity, and practicing stress-reduction techniques such as yoga or meditation.

Another way to build resilience is by developing a support system surrounding yourself with friends and loved ones. Having a supportive network of people who can provide emotional support, encouragement, and practical assistance can be a powerful buffer against stress and trauma.

It's also important to practice mindfulness and to be present in the moment. Mindfulness is the ability to be aware of one's thoughts, feelings, and bodily sensations in the present moment, without judgment. By practicing mindfulness, individuals can develop the ability to focus on the present and to let go of worries about the past or future.

Another important aspect of building resilience is learning to accept and embrace failure. As Thomas A. Edison once said, "I have not failed. I've just found 10,000 ways that won't work." Failure is a natural part of the learning and growth process, and it's important to view it as an opportunity for growth rather than a setback. By learning from our failures, we can gain insight into what works and what doesn't, and we can use that knowledge to inform our future decisions and actions. It's important to not give up and keep trying, because it's through failure that we learn and grow.

Finally, it's important to develop a sense of purpose and meaning. This might include things like volunteering, pursuing a passion or hobby, or connecting with a community or group that shares similar values and goals.

In conclusion, building resilience is an essential step in the healing process and moving forward. By taking care of oneself, developing a support system, practicing mindfulness, and finding purpose and meaning, individuals can develop the skills necessary to cope with difficult situations and to bounce back from adversity.

Part 3: Maintaining Mental Health and Wellness

Maintaining mental health and wellness is a critical aspect of healing from trauma and moving forward. The healing process is not a one-time event, but a lifelong journey, and it's important to have strategies in place for maintaining mental health and well-being.

One of the most important ways to maintain mental health and wellness is by continuing to work on one's emotional and psychological healing. This might include things like continuing to attend therapy or counseling, practicing self-care and self-compassion, and using coping strategies such as mindfulness, journaling, and exercise.

It's also important to prioritize self-care and self-compassion. This might include things like getting enough sleep, eating well, engaging in regular physical activity, and practicing stress-reduction techniques such as yoga or meditation.

Another key aspect of maintaining mental health and wellness is developing and maintaining a support system of friends, family, and loved ones. Having a strong support system can provide emotional support, encouragement, and practical assistance, and can help to buffer against stress and trauma.

It's also important to remember that taking control of one's life and being proactive in one's healing journey is crucial. As Stephen Hawking said, "Even people who claim that we can do nothing to change our destiny, look before crossing the street." We all have the ability to take steps to improve our well-being and to shape our own destinies. By being mindful of one's mental and emotional state, setting personal goals, and utilizing coping strategies, we can actively work towards healing and moving forward. It's important to remember that we are not passive participants in our own lives and that we have the power to make choices and take actions that will positively impact our mental health and well-being.

Finally, it's important to be mindful of one's mental and emotional state, and to be aware of the signs of stress and trauma. This might include things like feeling overwhelmed, anxious, or depressed, or experiencing physical symptoms such as headaches or stomachaches. Being aware of these signs can help individuals to take action before things get worse, and to seek help if necessary.

In conclusion, maintaining mental health and wellness is a critical aspect of the healing process and moving forward. By continuing to work on one's emotional and psychological healing, prioritizing self-care and self-compassion, developing and maintaining a support system, and being mindful of one's mental and emotional state, individuals can build resilience, find balance, and maintain well-being in the long-term.

In Conclusion

Healing from trauma is a difficult and complex process, but it is also possible. In this book, we have explored the link between trauma and anxiety, the different types of traumas, treatment options, coping strategies, and ways to move forward. We have discussed the importance of self-care and self-compassion, developing a support system, practicing mindfulness and meditation, journaling, exercise and physical activity, setting personal goals, and building resilience. We have also highlighted the importance of seeking professional help and the different types of therapy available.

We hope that this book has provided you with valuable insights and practical tools that can help you on your journey to healing and moving forward. Remember that healing is not a one-time event, but a lifelong journey. It's important to be kind and patient with yourself and to celebrate your progress, no matter how small.

We would like to remind you that healing from trauma is a process that may take time, and that it is important to seek professional help if you are struggling. Remember that you are not alone and that there are people who care and want to support you.

In the end, we hope that this book has helped you to understand that healing from trauma is possible. With the right tools, strategies, and support, you can overcome the challenges of trauma, and move forward with your life.

Resources and Recommended Reading

1. The Body Keeps the Score: Brain, Mind, and Body in the Healing of Trauma by Bessel van der Kolk
2. Trauma and Recovery: The Aftermath of Violence - From Domestic Abuse to Political Terror by Judith Herman
3. In an Unspoken Voice: How the Body Releases Trauma and Restores Goodness by Peter Levine
4. The Power of Now: A Guide to Spiritual Enlightenment by Eckhart Tolle
5. The Mindfulness Solution: Everyday Practices for Everyday Problems by Ronald D. Siegel
6. The Mindful Way Through Depression: Freeing Yourself from Chronic Unhappiness by Mark Williams, John Teasdale, Zindel Segal, and Jon Kabat-Zinn
7. The Anxiety and Phobia Workbook by Edmund J. Bourne
8. The Relaxation and Stress Reduction Workbook by Martha Davis, Elizabeth Robbins Eshelman, and Matthew McKay
9. The Healing Power of Mind: Simple Meditation Exercises for Health, Well-Being, and Enlightenment by Tulku Thondup
10. The Self-Compassion Workbook: A Proven Way to Accept Yourself, Build Inner Strength, and Thrive by Kristin Neff

Online Resources:

1. National Center for PTSD: www.ptsd.va.gov[1]
2. National Alliance on Mental Illness: www.nami.org[2]

---

1. http://www.ptsd.va.gov/

3. American Psychological Association: www.apa.org[3]
4. National Institute of Mental Health: www.nimh.nih.gov[4]
5. International Society for Traumatic Stress Studies: www.istss.org[5]
6. American Association for Marriage and Family Therapy: www.aamft.org[6]
7. International Association for Trauma Professionals: www.traumaassociates.com[7]
8. American Counseling Association: www.counseling.org[8]

Please note: This list of resources and recommended reading is not exhaustive and is intended as a starting point for further exploration and learning.

---

2. http://www.nami.org/

3. http://www.apa.org/

4. http://www.nimh.nih.gov/

5. http://www.istss.org/

6. http://www.aamft.org/

7. http://www.traumaassociates.com/

8. http://www.counseling.org/

Acknowledgments

I would like to express my deepest gratitude to my family for their unwavering support and encouragement throughout the writing of this book. I could not have done it without their love and support.

I would also like to thank my friends who have been by my side through the journey and who have provided me with their valuable feedback and support.

I am deeply grateful to my editor for their guidance, patience and for helping me to shape the manuscript into its final form.

I would like to acknowledge the work of the many researchers, therapists and professionals in the field of trauma and anxiety, who have contributed to the development of the concepts and techniques included in this book, without their passion to help others

Finally, I would like to thank my readers for their interest in this book and for their support. I hope that this book will help you to overcome your traumas and anxiety and to find peace.

About the Author

My name is Michael Ferguson, and I am the author of "Confronting Trauma and Overcoming Anxiety". I am a proud father, author and motivational coach with a passion for helping others to overcome the challenges of trauma and anxiety.

Like many people, I have my own personal experiences with trauma and anxiety. I understand the difficulties and struggles that come with it, and I know how hard it can be to find the right resources and support. But through my own journey of healing and self-discovery, I have come to realize the power of knowledge and understanding in overcoming these challenges.

This realization led me to embark on a journey of research and study, delving deep into the latest scientific research and therapeutic techniques for dealing with trauma and anxiety. I spent countless hours reading, studying and speaking with experts in the field, all in an effort to gain the knowledge and understanding necessary to help others.

The result of that journey is this book. My hope is that it will provide you with the information, tools and support you need to overcome your own traumas and anxieties and to find peace and happiness in your life.

I understand that everyone's journey is unique and different, but I believe that with the right tools and support, anyone can overcome their traumas and anxieties. I encourage you to read this book with an open mind and an open heart, and to trust in the power of knowledge and understanding to guide you on your journey to healing and self-discovery.

Thank you for reading, and I wish you all the best on your journey to confronting trauma and overcoming anxiety.

74

Don't miss out!

Visit the website below and you can sign up to receive emails whenever Michael Ferguson publishes a new book. There's no charge and no obligation.

https://books2read.com/r/B-A-CKNW-QZPEC

BOOKS 2 READ

Connecting independent readers to independent writers.

Did you love *Trauma To Triumph - A Journey To Overcoming Anxiety*? Then you should read *The Nuclear Threat of 2023: Understanding the Risks and Working Towards Disarmament*[1] by Michael Ferguson!

The Nuclear Threat of 2023 is a thought-provoking and eye-opening book that explores the terrifying possibility of a nuclear catastrophe in the near future. With the rise of global tensions and the proliferation of nuclear weapons, the world is facing unprecedented risks that demand urgent attention. This book provides a comprehensive analysis of the dangers posed by nuclear weapons, including the threat of accidental or intentional use, as well as the environmental

1. https://books2read.com/u/m2Q8Oo

2. https://books2read.com/u/m2Q8Oo

and humanitarian consequences of a nuclear detonation. It also offers a roadmap for disarmament and a vision for a safer, more peaceful world. Drawing on interviews with experts, policy makers, and activists, The Nuclear Threat of 2023 is an urgent call to action for anyone concerned about the future of humanity.